Cider Cocktails

Another Bite of the Apple

Darlene Hayes

photographs by Gregory Mast

Spotted Cat Press

Text copyright 2015 © Darlene Hayes
Photographs copyright 2015 © Gregory Mast
Photographs of apples generously provided by Bill Bleasdale, welshmountaincider.com

This book would not have been possible without the support of Jeffrey House of the California Cider Company, my dear friends Greg and Vernie Mast, and my wonderful husband Eric, who, among other things, drank a lot of cocktails, some of them very fast.

ISBN 978-0-9963215-0-1

Printed in Canada

Spotted Cat Press
P.O. Box 841
Graton, CA 94555-0841

CONTENTS

Introduction	4
Cocktails	7
Appetizers	39
Basic Recipes	60
Resources	62
Index	64

Introduction

Cider has a long history in the world. The British make it. The French make it. So do Spaniards and Germans. And Americans made it, lots of it, at least until that little hiccup called the Volstead Act introduced the dark decade or so of Prohibition. And while the word "cocktail" doesn't seem to have appeared until the early 19th century, cider mixed with spirits has probably been around for as long as cider and spirits. Nineteenth and early 20th century cocktail manuals, usually written by well respected bartenders, are full of cider-based drinks – punches and fizzes and toddies and more. Still, cider didn't bounce back into America's glasses until fairly recently. Now that it's easily available again, cider is finding its way into the creative tool box of many modern mixologists. And why not? Cider is made in a whole range of flavors and styles, at least in North America, providing ample opportunity to exploit its mixing possibilities.

Just to be clear, the cider I'm talking about isn't sweet juice. It is a fermented beverage made chiefly from apples or pears (in which case it is called perry). It can be still or sparkling, dry or sweet, and typically has at an alcohol content of around 6 - 7%, except for ice ciders whose concentrated sugars can bring them up to 10%.

Many ciders of the world are made using apples that you wouldn't care to eat because of their highly bitter tannin levels, but these same tannins can impart depth and complexity to a cider the way they do in a red wine. North American cider makers generally don't have access to much high-tannin fruit, though, since pre-Prohibition cider apple orchards were mostly torn out and replanted with other varieties. New orchards are going in, but in the meantime most cider makers have had to get a little creative and in doing so have come up with a style that some cider experts are calling New World.

New World Modern ciders are primarily made from the same apples you'd find in your average produce section – McIntosh, Gala, Jonagold, and the like. They are bright and refreshing and ofttimes tart. New World Heritage ciders are more likely to be made with apple varieties that were popular a hundred years ago, apples that served the dual purposes of cider making and eating such as Baldwin, Newtown Pippin, and Gravenstein. Heritage ciders will often be just a little more complex in flavor and will sometimes have a little tannin, and they may be just a bit more wine-like.

Many North American cider makers have also become innovative in the use of flavor adjuncts in their ciders, embracing barrel-aging, for example (for tannin, wood, and vanilla notes), and the addition of other fruits and botanicals such as hops and ginger. These imaginative permutations play right into the world of cocktails, where it's all about finding interesting combinations of flavors that stimulate both palate and conversation.

It may be useful to know just a little about the flavor profiles you would expect in ciders from other cider-producing countries, at least the major ones, as there are a number of North American cider makers that are emulating these styles. Ciders from the United Kingdom tend to be still, and most are made using apples containing a healthy dose of tannin. French ciders are also made with tannin-containing apples using a unique process that leaves them naturally sweet, very sparkling, and with an alcohol content closer to 4 - 5%. The peoples of Asturias and the Basque country in Spain (and southern France) have been making cider for millennia and have a style that is quite their own. The ciders are distinctly tart and still and are served by pouring small amounts from a height of several feet which aerates them, softening the acids a little, and giving them a fleeting mild fizz. German ciders, made mostly around Frankfurt, are also still and tart, and the modern ones are quite like a California Sauvignon Blanc.

There are just a few things to keep in mind when picking a cider to use in one of the recipes in this book. First there is carbonation. Most North American ciders are carbonated to at least some degree, and in most cases the absolute amount of fizz isn't critical to a cocktail and irrelevant in an appetizer. I've noted the few cases where you would really want to have either a cider that is still or particularly sparkling. Second there is residual sugar. You will find ciders described as dry, semi-dry, medium-dry, medium-sweet, and sweet. The truth is there is no labeling standard, so some ciders labeled as "dry" will still have significant sweetness and ciders labeled medium-dry that are sweet enough to compete with the sweetest soft drink. Most New World ciders will have a least a little sweetness as a way to balance the sharpness that comes from using eating apples, so I mostly suggest using what I would call a semi-dry cider – just a touch sweet. You'll probably have to give whatever cider you are thinking of using a try and go from there, but, really, the experiments are half the fun.

Wassail!

Cocktails

Stone Fence

The Stone Fence is easily one of the oldest cider concoctions on record dating back to at least the 18th century. It even played a small part in the American Revolution when Ethan Allen and his Green Mountain Boys spent the evening drinking the local version before setting off to take Fort Ticonderoga from the British. That would have been rum mixed with cider, for the Stone Fence is a flexible drink that makes use of whatever spirits, generally brown, might be at hand whether rum, rye, or bourbon. In my case, local means Spirit Works Sloe Gin and a local cider like Tilted Shed's Barred Rock Barrel Aged. I prefer using a cider than isn't bone dry, unless I'm mixing it with a good bourbon.

1 - 1 1/2 ounce spirits
4 - 5 ounces cider

Pour the spirits over ice, add the cider and stir.

Gin Gin Jenny

If this drink reminds you of a gin and tonic, it should, but its inspiration is the Gin Gin (gin and ginger beer), which is a variation on the Moscow Mule. Ginger and apple are a natural pair, and there are many ginger-infused ciders to choose from. Two of my particular favorites when making this cocktail are Reverend Nat's Ginger Tonic (which gets a little of that G & T thing going) and Finnriver's Forrest Ginger, which is made with fir tips in addition to the ginger. Something about the resiny notes contributed by the fir embraces the botanical flavors of the gin and takes them both to a new level.

2 ounces gin
5 ounces ginger cider
1/4 lime

Pour the gin into an ice-filled glass, add the cider and give it a stir. Squeeze in the lime and stir again.

Stone Fence

Orleans Fizz

Orleans Fizz

Fizzes have been around since the 19th century, the most famous being the Ramos Fizz. Some include a carbonated component, some have just egg, but all end up being fun and frothy. In this variation we get fizz from both sides ramped up by one of the amazing aperitif ciders made by Vermont's Eden Ice Cider, in this case Orleans Herbal. If that proves impossible to find, try substituting another herb-infused aperitif like Lillet® or Dubonnet®. Then find a cider you like that has lots of bubbles, not too dry.

1 1/2 ounces gin
2 ounces Orleans Herbal
1 egg white
1 Tbsp cream
1 tsp lime juice
4 ounces semi-dry sparkling cider

Place the first 5 ingredients in a shaker with some ice. Shake very well for several minutes. Strain into an ice-filled glass, then quickly top with the sparkling cider.

Rose's Smile

The antecedent to this cocktail, the Royal Smile, first appeared in the early 20th century. Robert Vermeire, a well respected barman at London's Embassy Club, describes it in his 1922 classic book Cocktails, How to Mix Them *with the note that it is improved by the addition of a little cream. He was right, although the result is a rather alarming pink. I've taken the modifications a bit further by replacing the original apple brandy with still cider, making the whole thing a little less boozy. The still ciders made by Farnum Hill or Virtue have the good strong tannins that give this cocktail an extra depth.*

2 ounces gin
1 ounce still cider
1 Tbsp cream
1 tsp grenadine
juice of 1/2 lime

Place all the ingredients in a shaker with ice, then shake well to cool and blend. Strain into a martini glass.

Honey Buzz

Cider fermented with honey is called cyser and even when fermented to complete dryness retains some of the unique flavor of the honey. The California Cider Company's Ace Honey is a good example as is Blissful Moon made by Harvest Moon cidery in New York. It's hard to beat the flavors of honey and coffee together, especially if you like a cocktail on the sweeter side.

1 1/2 ounces vodka
1 ounce Kalúa®
4 ounces honey cider or cyser

Combine the vodka and Kalúa® in a glass with some ice. Stir to chill, then strain into another glass and add the cider. Add a little more ice to keep the cocktail nice and cold.

Ruby Tuesday

I have been making this cocktail using blood orange juice, which has an interesting spicy edge not found in regular oranges, and calling it a Ruby Tuesday for its rich, red color. Blood orange juice is hard to come by when they're not in season, but use it if you can. The real key to this cocktail, though, is the Eden Ice Cider Orleans Bitter, which adds a wonderful complexity, and the touch of tart sweetness from the ice cider.

1 1/2 ounces vodka
2 1/2 ounces Orleans Bitter
2 1/2 ounces orange juice
1/2 ounce ice cider
1/2 tsp grenadine

Combine everything in a shaker with some ice, then shake well to blend and chill. Strain into a martini glass.

Honey Buzz

Barberrian

Barberrian

We grow a lot of berries in the western states, so it is only natural that berries of all kinds have found their way into western ciders – raspberries (Cider Riot, WA), marionberries (Two Towns, OR), blackberries (Ace. CA), huckleberries (Two Rivers, CA), and blueberries (Julian Hard Cider, CA). All work well in this cocktail. The surprise came when one day I was out of berry cider and so tried Two Towns Rhubarbarian instead. The tart rhubarb worked just as well here as it does in a strawberry rhubarb pie, with the added bonus of just a little astringency to liven things up.

1 ounce vodka
1/2 ounce Cointreau®
1/4 ounce lemon juice
4 - 5 ounces berry or rhubarb cider
fresh berries as a garnish

Combine the first three ingredients in a shaker with some ice, shake to blend and chill, then pour into a martini glass. Add the cider and some berries as a garnish.

Berry Storm

Many ports have a pronounced berry character, especially those made in northern California, but they are too rich and intense on their own to work well as a cocktail. The addition of vodka moderates some of that richness and the berry cider brings down the intensity while simultaneously adding another layer of flavor.

1 ounce vodka
2 ounces port
1 tsp curaçao
1 tsp lemon juice
4 - 5 ounces berry cider

Add the first four ingredients to a glass of ice, then stir for a bit to both blend and chill. Strain the mixture into a second glass of ice, then top with the berry cider.

Cider Nectar

Recipes for Cider Nectar go back to at least 1862 with the publication of America's first book of cocktails How to Mix Drinks, or, The Bon-vivant's Companion *by Jerry Thomas. Most recipes call for brandy and sherry, and sherry is nice, but rum plays especially well off the pineapple cider. Of course, pineapple cider was unheard of in 1862, but I like to think that 19th century bartenders would have welcomed it with open arms.*

1 ounce brandy
1 ounce dark rum
2 tsp lemon juice
2 tsp simple syrup (page 60)
3 ounces pineapple cider
pineapple for garnish

Mix the brandy, rum, lemon juice, and simple syrup in a shaker with some ice. Shake well, strain into a glass, then add the cider and a little ice. Garnish with a pineapple spear if you have good ripe pineapple.

Revolution No. 3

The renewed interest in cocktails has created all manner of opportunities for entrepreneurial types to make and market creative and delicious artisanal mixers. The ladies at Owl's Brew have based theirs in tea freshly brewed with interesting additional flavors from various herbs and spices, then sweetened just a bit to give some balance. Pink and Black starts with Darjeeling tea, then adds hibiscus, lemon peel, strawberry, and agave. The tannins in the tea give the drink an extra edge.

1 1/2 ounce dark rum
1 1/2 ounces Owl's Brew Pink and Black
juice from 1/4 lime
6 ounces dry or semi-dry cider

Mix everything together and serve over ice.

Cider Nectar

Cot Dreamin'

Apricots are a wonder of nature, at once honey sweet and pleasingly tart. The same could be said of this cocktail, with a little earthy nuttiness from the Amaretto thrown in. Apricot ciders aren't as easy to find as some others (Tieton Cider Works makes a good one as does Reverend Nat), so if you can't find one you might try substituting a honey cider and adding another half an apricot. Fresh apricots out of season? You can happily use canned apricots (in light syrup).

1 ounce dark rum
1/2 ounce amaretto
2 whole apricots
1 Tbsp orange juice
1 tsp lemon juice
1 tsp simple syrup (page 60)
4 ounces apricot cider

Blend the rum, Amaretto, apricots, orange and lemon juices, and simple syrup in a blender until smooth. Pour the mixture into the cider. Serve in a martini glass.

Mekong Melody

The great Mekong river originates high on the Tibetan plateau, touching a handful of countries as it winds its way to the South China Sea. While each of these countries has a distinct cuisine they share a palate made up of flavors hot, sour, salty, and sweet. This sounds like a wonderful jumping off point for a cocktail based on one of the handful of spicy ciders on the market (for example Seattle Cider's Three Pepper, Finnriver's Habañero, and Schilling Cider's Sriracha Lime). Absent one of these, try adding a bit of Sriracha to your favorite semi-dry cider or add a few thai chilis when you crush the basil and kaffir lime leaves.

8 - 10 fresh thai basil leaves
1 kaffir lime leaf
1 1/2 ounces dark rum
3/4 tsp simple syrup (page 60)
juice of 1/4 lime
1/8 tsp fish sauce
6 ounces pepper cider

Crush the leaves in a shaker, add a handful of ice plus the next four ingredients. Shake well, strain over ice, then stir in the cider.

J.P. Hill

John Philip Hill, congressman for the fine state of Maryland from 1921 to 1927, wanted to sell 2.75% beer. Thus, in 1924 he set out to challenge the Volstead Act by fermenting cider and serving it quite publicly. There was, you see, a part of the law that allowed for the private making of "nonintoxicating cider and fruit juice" without defining "nonintoxicating." Hill was indicted, went to trial, and was acquitted because the jury found his fully fermented (probably) 7% cider to be "nonintoxicating in fact." The ruling let wineries stay afloat through Prohibition by selling grapes to home wine makers, though, alas, it didn't save many cider apple orchards. Hill never did get to sell any 2.75% beer, but he certainly deserves a cocktail.

1 - 2 ounces rye
1 ounce peach purée
1 tsp simple syrup (page 60)
5 ounces dry cider

Combine the rye, purée, and simple syrup in a shaker with ice. Shake well, the strain and add the cider. Add some ice, too, if you like.

Virginia Reel

Virginians have been making cider since the first colonists arrived in the 17th century, even developing their own regional cider apple favorites like the Hewes Crabapple. This cocktail acknowledges early Virginia's Scottish settlers and their rich distilling history, with a nod to modern Virginia cider makers, such as Blue Bee and Potter's Craft, who are dipping their toes in the waters of modern American cider by adding hops. The hickory syrup enhances the smokiness of the scotch, but if you can't find any try using maple syrup in its place.

3/4 ounce scotch
3/4 ounce applejack
1 1/2 tsp hickory syrup
3 ounces hopped cider

Shake the scotch, applejack, and hickory syrup in a shaker with a few ice cubes to blend and chill. Strain into a glass, stir in the cider, then add a few more ice cubes.

J.P. Hill

Pumpkin Cider Toddy

Pumpkin Cider Toddy

Who doesn't love a hot toddy on a frozen winter night or when in the pernicious clutches le rheum? The honey soothes, the lemon adds a dash of vitamin C, and the spirits both warm and send us into a pleasant reverie. Most recipes call for boiling water in the mix, but how much better to use cider instead. The popular seasonal pumpkin cider is a natural here, but your favorite semi-dry apple cider would work nicely, too.

1 ounce applejack or brandy
1 1/2 Tbsp honey
1 Tbsp lemon juice
6 ounces pumpkin cider
1 cinnamon stick
grated nutmeg (optional)

Put the applejack or brandy, lemon juice and honey in your favorite mug. Heat the cider and cinnamon stick until it just comes to a boil, then pour it into the mug and stir until the honey dissolves. Add a little nutmeg if you are so inclined. Drink in front of a nice fire or under a downy comforter.

Jersey Lightning

Distilled apple spirits have a venerable history in the U.S. with Laird and Co. opening the first American commercial distillery in New Jersey in 1780. Eight generations later the family is still at it. This particular cocktail probably originates from the early 19th century when modern bitters became popular. Try making the sugar syrup with demerara sugar, which will add more depth of flavor. It's a potent drink, so I add a bit of cider to lighten it up.

2 ounces applejack
1/2 ounce simple syrup (page 60)
2 dashes orange bitters
a splash of dry or semi-dry cider
1 piece of orange rind

Stir all the liquid ingredients together and pour over ice. Garnish with the orange peel.

Dr. Walker

Eighteenth century Virginian Dr. Thomas Walker was not quite the renaissance man that his good friend Peter Jefferson's son Thomas was, but he was a dedicated explorer (into what would later become Kentucky) and a respected surgeon. More importantly, he was the champion of one of the colonies' best new apple varieties, the Newtown Pippin, which became the Albemarle Pippin when he and T. Jefferson planted it on their Virginia estates. Modern cider makers from east (Albemarle Ciderworks) to west (Colorado Cider Co.) have embraced its bright crispness. Why add persimmon? Well just because early Virginia colonists made a respectable fermented drink from the indigenous fruit.

1 1/2 - 2 ounces bourbon
2 ounces persimmon purée
3 tsp honey
3 ounces tart, dry cider

Shake the first three ingredients together with some ice, mix in the cider, then strain into a martini glass.

The Methodist

Another simple and tasty 19th century cocktail was the Presbyterian – scotch and ginger ale – although no one seems to remember how it got the name. My mother, though, was a lifelong Methodist. She grew up in the thick of the temperance movement and in all the time I knew her never touched a drop of alcohol. Still, she went through a period in the early 1950s where she liked drinking Manhattans and dancing with the fellows at the local USO. So, here's to you, Mom.

1 ounce bourbon
4 ounces ginger cider
a piece of lemon peel

Mix the bourbon and cider together, add ice, then twist the lemon peel over the top of the drink so that it is nicely sprayed with lemon oil.

Ume Hana

Rescue Remedy

Spend any time reading through old drinks and/or cider-making manuals and you will discover that alcoholic preparations have a long use as medicinals. Concoctions such as "Nervous Head Medicine" and "Spinster's Nightcap" abound. John Worlidge's Vinum Britanicum: Or a Treatise of Cider and Other Wines and Drinks *(1691) while praising cider as a perfect beverage also suggests that it can be a wonderful medium for delivering the medicinal properties of various herbs and spices perhaps giving new depth to the toast "to your health!"*

1 1/2 ounces rye
1/2 ounce spiced syrup (page 61)
4 ounces dry cider

Stir the rye and spiced syrup together until fully incorporated, then add the cider. Serve over ice.

Ume Hana

Shochu is not a spirit that shows up in western cocktails much, but it's pretty popular in its native stomping ground of Japan. Distilled from fermented barley or rice, it has an interesting earthiness that is simultaneously clean. Add some sweet fruity notes from the plum wine, a little bit of savoriness from the salty umeboshi paste, and a spicy zing from ginger cider (Schilling Cider's is one of my favorites) and you are ready for a night on the town in Tokyo.

1 1/2 ounce shochu
2 ounces plum wine
1/8 tsp umeboshi paste
6 ounces ginger cider

Add the shochu, plum wine, and umeboshi paste to a shaker with some ice, then shake vigorously to blend the paste into the liquids. Strain into an ice-filled glass and add the ginger cider.

Maggie May

Nothing says "fun" like a margarita, and few classic cocktails are as ripe for variation. Start with tequila, add something fruity, something tart, something sweet, and you are off to the races.

2 ounces tequila
4 ounces frozen strawberries
3/4 ounce Chambord®
1/2 ounce triple sec
1/4 ounce white balsamic vinegar
3 ounces berry cider

Place the tequila, strawberries, Chambord®, triple sec, and vinegar in a blender and process until completely smooth. Add the cider, give it a quick pulse, then pour into a martini or margarita glass.

Cocoa Hop

Hops and chocolate are natural favor partners so it's surprising that they aren't used together more often. Hops can also add a lot to a cider, especially one made principally from apples that don't have much in the way of tannin. That edge of bitterness and rich aroma can lend depth to a cider that might otherwise be a little ordinary. It should be no surprise that many delightful hopped ciders come from the northwest – they do, after all, grow an awful lot of hops there. Ciders from Anthem, Tieton, and Finnriver are a few personal favorites.

1 1/2 ounces tequila
1 ounce crème de cacao
4 ounces hopped cider

Stir the tequila and crème de cacao together in a glass, then add the cider and a handful of ice.

Maggie May

Midnight Sun

Spicy Swede

Aquavit doesn't appear much in historic American cocktails, which is a bit of a surprise as there have certainly been plenty of immigrants from Scandinavia who would have likely brought their local spirits with them. It's gained more traction as a cocktail ingredient in recent years, and a good thing, too, as the mix of herbs and spices used to give aquavit its character, chiefly caraway, can bring a lot to the flavor party. Here its paired with a zing of fresh ginger juice and mellowed a bit by the cider.

1 1/2 ounce aquavit
1 tsp simple syrup (page 60)
1 - 2 inch piece of fresh ginger
8 ounces semi-dry cider

Put the aquavit and simple syrup into a shaker. Make some ginger juice by finely grating the ginger, then squeezing out its liquid. Add about 1/2 tsp to the shaker, along with some ice, and shake well to blend. Pour over ice, then add the cider and give it all a quick stir.

Midnight Sun

Cherries, tart and sweet, are a fine addition to cider. Cider makers across America certainly agree as cherry ciders are being produced from New York (like Original Sin Cherry Tree) to Oregon (like Blue Mountain Cherry) and a dozen places in between. Cherries are also a great match with caraway, which makes cherry cider a natural for blending with aquavit.

1 ounce aquavit
1/2 tsp simple syrup (page 60)
6 ounces cherry cider
1/8 fresh lime

Combine the aquavit, simple syrup, and cherry cider in a glass, then squeeze in the lime juice.

Black Velvet

The Black Velvet dates to 1861 London when Great Britain was mourning the death of Price Albert, Queen Victoria's prince consort. It consisted of a layer of champagne topped with a layer of stout (the dark layer symbolized a black armband). Those who didn't have the means to afford champagne could order the drink with cider or beer instead, whereupon it was renamed a Poor Man's Black Velvet. I seen no reason to denigrate a perfectly lovely drink. And since the whole layering process is a little fussy, symbolism notwithstanding, I've dropped that, too. You can use just about any cider, but I like it best with one that is sparkling and semi-dry.

6 ounces good stout
6 ounces cider

Pour the cider into the glass first, then add the stout so that it forms a nice rich head.

Cidre Royale

The marriage of white wine and cassis, or kir, is a classic from the mid-19th century. Mix cassis with champagne and you get a Kir Royale. Mix it with cider and you get a Cidre Royale. Whatever the name, this is an acknowledged classic, at once simple and sophisticated. Swap the cassis for a raspberry liqueur and you have Cidre Framboise. Or add a dash of calvados if you've had a hard day. Just use a cider that is clean and sparkling, dry or sweet. I particularly like using a barrel-aged cider such as Virtue Cider's The Mitten or Traditions Ciderwork's Bourbon Barrel. The vanilla flavors from the barrel work brilliantly with the cassis.

2 tsp crème de cassis
6 - 7 ounces cider

Put the crème de cassis in the bottom of a champagne or wine glass, then pour in the cider.

Cidre Royale

Architect's Fancy

Architect's Fancy

One of the regulars at a local cider tasting room down the road has often mentioned that he likes nibbling on a stalk of wild fennel while he's sipping a glass of cider and has repeatedly suggested that the cider maker there figure out how to combine the two flavors. In fact, he's on to something, especially if the cider in question is a pear cider (apple-based cider flavored with pears) or perry. A hint of orange brings it all together.

1 1/2 ounce ouzo
2 tsp curaçao
8 ounces pear cider or perry

Mix the ouzo and cider in a glass. Add some ice and the pear cider and give it a bit of a stir.

Negroni Piegato

The classic negroni cocktail blends gin, vermouth, and Compari®. Swap out the gin for Prosecco and you get a Negroni Sbagliato, Italian for "broken." Going with a lighter alcohol doesn't seem so much broken to me as maybe a little bent (piegato). You'll want to use a bright, sparkling cider here like First Fruits from Foggy Ridge in Virginia.

1/2 ounce Campari®
1/2 ounce sweet vermouth
5 ounces dry sparkling cider
1 small piece of lemon peel

Stir the liquids together, then pour into glass, on the rocks or not. Twist the lemon peel over the top, then use it to garnish the drink.

Gen. Harrison's Nog

General William Henry Harrison, America's 9th president, may have lasted only a month or so in office, but he did manage to contribute a his bit to the history of cider. During his 1840 campaign, his opponents tried to paint him as out of touch, just sitting in his log cabin drinking cider. Harrison and his running mate, both from aristocratic families, welcomed this chance to connect with the common man, so they embraced the imagery and began handing out cider in log cabin-shaped bottles at every campaign event. They won in a landslide. This nog, it's said, was General Harrison's favorite drink.

1 egg
4 ounces still cider
1 1/2 tsp brown sugar
2 tsp cream
grated nutmeg to garnish

Break the egg into a shaker and beat lightly to break it up. Add the cider, sugar, cream, and a few ice cubes, then shake vigorously for several minutes. Strain into a glass and garnish with grated nutmeg.

Spring Cider Punch

Punches first appeared in 17th century England, arriving with returning members of the British East India Company. Popular at parties, punches generally contained some sort of fruit element and were understood to be a little less alcoholic, the better to drink and dance all night. Early drinks manuals describe any number of punches using cider, but I've let my own imagination be the driver of this one – sherry for nuttiness, Lillet® for herbal complexity, and elderflower liqueur for its wonderful floral aroma. The amounts are for a single glassful, of course, so if you are planning on making enough for a crowd, you'll need to do a little arithmetic.

1/2 ounce Lillet®
1/2 ounce elderflower liqueur
1/2 ounce orange juice
2 tsps sherry
5 ounces dry cider
orange slice for garnish

Mix all of the ingredients together. Serve over a little ice with an orange slice as a garnish.

Spring Cider Punch

Appetizers

Mushroom and Walnut Spread

Cider adds a bright acidity to the rich mushrooms and walnuts that are the backbone of this spread. To make a vegan version, use a vegan cream cheese or leave it out all together. You probably won't miss it.

1 3/4 cup dry cider
1 1/4 ounce mixed dried mushrooms (porcini and shitake)
1/2 ounce dried apple pieces
1 Tbsp olive oil
10 ounces fresh button mushrooms, quartered
1 clove garlic, peeled and minced
2 tsp fresh thyme, minced
3 ounces walnut pieces, toasted
1 Tbsp white miso
1 ounce cream cheese
1 tsp ground black pepper
1/4 tsp salt or to taste
2 tsp minced shallot as a garnish (optional)

Bring the cider to a boil, then add the dried mushrooms and apples. Cover, remove from the heat and let steep for 1 - 2 hours.

Heat the olive oil in a large skillet over medium heat, then add the fresh mushrooms, garlic, and thyme. Cook, stirring occasionally, until the mushrooms are soft. Add the soaked dried mushrooms and apples along with the soaking liquid. Raise the heat, then simmer until the liquid is completely gone.

Let the mushroom mixture cool a bit, then place in a food processor along with walnuts, miso, cream cheese, and black pepper. Process in pulses until you've achieved a smooth paste. Check the seasoning and add salt to taste.

Store chilled for at least 2 hours before serving to let all of the flavors develop. Serve with bread or crackers.

Makes about 2 cups

Braised Meatballs

Robust and full-flavored, you can also use these meatballs over pasta. Just don't cook away quite so much of the braising liquid. You can use either a dry or semi-dry cider in the braise.

1 1/4 lbs ground lamb or beef
1 medium onion, peeled
1 large egg
1/2 cup dried bread crumbs
1/2 tsp ground allspice
3 1/4 tsp salt
1 tsp ground black pepper
2 Tbsps olive oil
8 garlic cloves, peeled
1/2 cup cider
1/4 cup beef stock
1 cup crushed canned tomatoes
1 Tbsp tomato paste
1 Tbsp cider vinegar
1 bouquet garni (page 61)
2 Tbsp butter
2 tsp minced parsley as a garnish

Mix the ground meat, onion, egg, bread crumbs, allspice, 1 1/2 tsp of salt, and 1 tsp of black pepper together until thoroughly blended. Pinch off walnut-size bits of the meat mixture and roll into balls (this is easier to do with wet hands).

Heat the oil in a large skillet, then brown the meatballs in batches, setting aside those that have browned while you cook the next batch.

While the meatballs are browning, cut the garlic cloves into quarters. When the last of the meatballs is almost done, add the garlic to the pan and let the pieces brown a bit, too. Add the cider and let it come to a simmer while scraping up any browned bits on the bottom of the pan. Add the rest of the ingredients except the butter, salt, and pepper and the parsley. Cover and slowly simmer 30 - 40 minutes, then uncover, raise the heat and cook until most of the braising liquid cooks away. Stir in the butter, spoon into a serving bowl, then garnish with the parsley.

Makes 3 dozen meatballs

Cider Poached Shrimp

Poaching in cider is a popular way to cook fish and shellfish in France's cider-making regions. The cider give the fish a subtle, pleasant fruitiness, especially a cider with a little sweetness.

1 cup semi-dry cider
1 bouquet garni (page 61)
3/4 tsp salt
1 1/4 tsp ground black pepper
1 lb jumbo shrimp (about 24)
3 cloves garlic, peeled and minced
1/4 cup finely chopped onion
1 Tbsp olive oil
3/4 cup chopped canned tomatoes
2 tsp prepared horseradish
2 tsp crème fraîche (page 61)
1 tsp minced chives as a garnish

Bring the cider, bouquet garni, 1/2 tsp of salt, and 1/4 tsp of black pepper to a simmer. Add the shrimp, cover, lower the heat, and cook just until the shrimp are cooked through, about 5 minutes. Remove the shrimp, saving the liquid, set them aside, let them cool, then refrigerate until you are ready to serve them. They can be poached a day ahead to time.

To make the dipping sauce, heat the olive oil in a small pan and cook the garlic and onion until soft and a little translucent. Add the tomatoes and poaching liquid (along with the bouquet garni), raise the heat and simmer vigorously until most of the liquid is gone and the mixture is quite thick. Turn off the heat and let cool for a bit, then blend in a blender until very smooth. Stir in the horseradish and créme fraiche. Check the seasoning, adding more salt and pepper if you think it needs it. Chill several hours before serving to let the flavors marry.

Makes about 2 dozen

Cherry Chutney Timbale

Spread between layers of a goat cheese/cream cheese mixture, this chutney makes a find appetizer, but you can also use it on its own as a sweet/tart accompaniment to roasted duck or lamb. Use a berry cider if you can't find cherry.

For the chutney:
2 1/2 tsp yellow mustard seeds
1 cup dried Bing cherries
1/3 cup finely minced onion
1 large garlic clove, finely minced
1 1/4 cup cherry cider
1/4 cup red wine vinegar
1/4 cup packed brown sugar
1 tsp minced fresh rosemary
1 tsp minced fresh thyme
1 tsp ground black pepper
1 pinch salt

Lightly toast the mustard seeds in a small pan, then crush them a bit. Chop the dried cherries as finely as you can. Combine all the ingredients in one pot, bring to a simmer, cover, then cook over low heat for 20 - 30 minutes. Uncover the pot, raise the heat, and cook until all of the liquid has evaporated or been absorbed.

Cool, then refrigerate for at least 3 days to let the flavors come together. Makes 1 cup of chutney.

For the timbale:
8 ounces fresh goat cheese
4 ounces cream cheese
1/4 tsp salt
1 pinch ground black pepper

Let the two cheeses sit at room temperature until softened, then blend together along with the salt and pepper.

To make the timbale, line a 16-ounce bowl with plastic wrap, then create alternating layers of cheese and chutney, beginning and ending with the cheese. Cover and chill. Serve with crackers or sliced baguette rounds.

Serves 12 - 15

Savory Artichokes

I usually use a dry cider when making this dish, but a semi-dry would be nice, too. Do use one that doesn't have much in the way of tannin. The artichokes have enough bitter elements themselves. If you can find fresh artichokes, by all means use them.

1 1/2 lbs fresh baby artichokes or
  8 ounces frozen artichoke hearts
1 large clove garlic, peeled
2 sprigs fresh parsley
2 springs fresh rosemary
2 sprigs fresh thyme
1 lemon cut into 8ths plus a second
  if you are using fresh artichokes
1 1/2 cups cider
1/2 tsp salt
1/4 tsp ground black pepper
1/4 cup good fruity olive oil

If you are using fresh artichokes, fill a bowl half-way with cold water, then cut up the extra lemon, squeeze its juice into the water, then add in the lemon halves in as well. Clean the artichokes by snapping off the tough outer leaves one at a time at the base until you reach the tender pale yellow inside leaves. Cut off the top half of the leaves and discard. Use a knife or vegetable peeler to pare away the tough ends of the leaves left on the heart. Cut the heart in half and scoop out any bristly bits you see in the center. Cut the halves in half again, then toss them into the bowl of water while you clean the rest of the artichokes.

If you are using frozen artichoke hearts, just thaw them.

Combine the artichokes, freshly cleaned or thawed, in a pot with the garlic, herbs, cut up lemon, and cider. Simmer, covered, until the artichokes are tender, about 15 or 20 minutes. Uncover the pot, raise the heat, and simmer until most of the liquid has evaporated. Stir in the salt, pepper, and olive oil. Chill, but serve closer to room temperature.

Makes about 3 cups of artichokes

Spanish Chorizo Bites

The Asturians of northern Spain have been making cider longer than anyone in the world, so it's no mystery that they also cook with it. This chorizo dish is one you will often find in an Asturian cider restaurant or sideria. Use the tartest, driest cider you can find.

1 medium onion
1 Tbsp fruity olive oil
8 ounces dry Spanish chorizo
3/4 cup tart, dry cider
1/4 tsp ground black pepper
1 large pinch of salt if needed

Peel and quarter the onion, then cut it into thin slices. Heat the olive oil in a pan over medium heat, and cook the onion until it is soft and translucent.

While the onion is cooking, cut the chorizo into 1/2 inch rounds, then cut each round in half. Add the chorizo to the pan with the onion and cook for 5 minutes, stirring occasionally. Add the cider, cover the pan, lower the heat to medium low, and cook for 20 minutes.

Uncover, the pan, raise the heat to high, and simmer until most of the liquid has cooked away. Stir in the salt and pepper. Serve warm with toothpicks.

Makes 1 1/2 cups of chorizo

Celery Root Rémoulade in Endive Leaves

This is a fine, classic French salad all on its own, and you can turn it into a nicely refreshing canapé by piling it into fresh Belgian endive leaves. The secret to its snappy flavor is the cider mustard, which has an infinite number of uses in its own right.

For the rémoulade:
1 lb celery root
1/2 tsp salt
1 generous Tbsp cider mustard
1/4 cup mayonnaise
1/4 tsp ground black pepper
3 - 4 tsp minced wild arugula or parsley
3 - 4 Belgian endives

Peel the celery root, then cut it into fine matchstick-sized pieces, or you can coarsely grate it. Place into a strainer, then sprinkle in the salt, mixing it in with your hands. Let the celery root sit at room temperature for 20 - 25 minutes while the salt draws out some of the moisture and softens the celery root.

Quickly rinse the celery root under running water, then squeeze out as much moisture as you can using your hands. Put the celery root in a bowl with the next four ingredients, and mix thoroughly. Chill for several hours.

To serve, peel off the larger outer leaves of the endive and fill with the rémoulade.

For the cider mustard:
1/3 cup black mustard seeds
2 Tbsp cider vinegar
1/2 cup cider
1 1/4 tsp salt

Combine all the ingredients in a bowl and let them sit overnight. The next day, put the soaked seeds and any unabsorbed liquid in a blender and blend well. Put the mustard through a fine strainer to remove the bitter hulls. Let sit 24 hours for the best flavor.

Makes about 3/4 cup mustard and 2 dozen canapés

Roasted Chicken Rillettes

Rillettes are meat spreads that tend to the fatty. This one is meatier than most, and the tangy cider gives it a welcome brightness. Sealed with a layer of duck fat, you can store this spread in a cold part of your refrigerator for at least a month.

1 3 1/2 lb chicken, roasted and cooled
1 leek, white part only
1 medium carrot, peeled
1/2 medium onion
1 clove garlic, unpeeled
1 small bunch parsley stems
3 sprigs fresh thyme
1 cup semi-dry cider
1 Tbsp duck fat or butter
1/4 cup minced shallot
1/4 cup dry cider

Strip the skin and meat from the chicken and set aside. Coarsely chop the leek, carrot, and onion. Put the chicken bones, chopped vegetables, garlic, parsley stems, and thyme in a pot with the semi-dry cider and 1 cup of water. Bring to a simmer, cover, and cook gently for 1 hour. Strain and discard the solids.

Heat the duck fat in a large skillet, then add the shallots and cook over medium-low heat until they are soft and translucent. Meanwhile, separate out the chicken skin and 2 cups of meat (save the rest for another use). Mince the skin, then add it, and the 2 cups of meat, to the skillet with the shallots. Add the bone broth and the 1/4 cup of dry cider. Simmer over medium heat until virtually all of the liquid is gone.

Transfer the chicken to a bowl and let it begin to cool. While it is still warm work it with a wooden spoon, stirring and breaking up the chicken until you have created a spreadable mass. Check it for seasoning, adding salt and/or pepper if you think it needs it. Chill overnight. Return to room temperature at least 1 hour before serving.

Makes about 2 cups

Dried Apricot Chutney

Like its cherry cousin (page 46), this chutney can do double duty as a condiment for roasted meats, especially chicken or pork. As part of a cheese platter, it shines when spread over a tangy blue cheese and served along with some marcona almonds.

4 ounces dried apricots
1 ounce dried apples
1 1/4 cup dry cider
1/2 cup packed brown sugar
2 Tbsp cider vinegar
1/4 cup thinly sliced onion
1 small dried red chili
1 large pinch of salt
1/2 tsp dry mustard powder

Cut the dried apricots into quarters, or 1/2 inches pieces if the apricots are large. Finely chop the dried apple. Put the dried fruits in a pot along with the rest of the ingredients, and bring to a simmer. Cover and simmer gently for 30 minutes, then uncover, raise the heat a little, and cook until the chutney is very thick and glossy. Let the chutney cool, then remove the chili. The flavor will be more developed if you let it sit for a day or so before using it.

Makes about 1 1/2 cups

Onion Confit Canapés

There are so many ways to use this onion confit (a sort of savory jam). Serve it warm along side roast beef or steak. Pile it on top of a whole brie cheese, then bake until the brie is a little melted. Or use it for a topping to cheese and crackers as I've done here.

3 large onions, about 1 1/4 lbs
2 Tbsps butter
2 sprigs fresh thyme, or 3/4 tsp dried thyme leaves
2/3 cup dry or semi-dry cider
1 large pinch of piment d'espelette or cayenne pepper
1/2 tsp salt
assorted cheeses such as brie or gouda
crackers
green herbs for garnish (optional)

Peel the onions, quarter them, then slice them thinly. Melt the butter in a large frying pan over low heat, then add the onions and the thyme. Cook very gently until the onions are golden and caramelized, about 50 to 60 minutes. Stir occasionally at first, then more often so that the onions color evenly and don't stick to the pan.

Add the cider and the piment d'espelette or cayenne, then raise the heat to medium high. Cook, stirring frequently, until the liquid has reduced to almost nothing. Stir in the salt (check to make sure it doesn't need a little more). Let the confit cool, then refrigerate until ready to use.

Makes about 1 cup of confit

For the canapés, bring the confit to room temperature. Slice the cheese, place on a cracker, then top with 1 heaping tsp of confit. Garnish with some green herbs, like chopped parsley, if you like.

Basic Recipes

Simple Syrup

Simple syrup is nothing more than sugar in water. Sugar is much quicker to dissolve in hot liquid rather than cold, and since cocktails by their very nature are generally cold, you can waste a lot of time getting that little hit of sweet in your drink, time much better spent doing almost anything else. It will last quite a while in your refrigerator, so don't hesitate to make enough to last a while.

Here's the fun part about simple syrup. You don't need to just use white cane sugar. You can add a whole separate level of flavor to your drink by using brown sugar, or even demerara, muscovado, or turbinado sugars, all of which have more residual molasses in them than brown sugar and so will give you an even richer flavor. I almost always use a simple syrup made from demerara or turbinado sugar when making cocktails using barrel-aged spirits like bourbon, brandy, applejack, whisky, and dark rum.

Simple syrups can be made in varying ratios of sugar to water. For the ones used in this book I stick to 2 parts sugar to one part water since I see no point in diluting my drink unnecessarily.

1/2 cup sugar
1/4 cup water

Put the water and sugar in a pan and heat, stirring, just until the sugar has completely dissolved. Let cool, then store in the refrigerator until needed.

Makes just over 1/2 cup

Spiced Simple Syrup

Sweet spiced wine, aka Hippocras, was popular from the height of the Roman Empire into the 18th century when it more or less disappeared but for the occasional holiday glüwein. The spices in Hippocras were thought to possess medicinal and even aphrodisiac properties, which may account for its popularity. While I can't vouch for any of that, I can say that it makes a pretty tasty addition to the right drink.

1/2 cup turbinado sugar
1/3 cup water
2 tsps cardamom
1 tsp grains of paradise
1 tsp whole cloves
3 Balinese long peppers
3 1/4 inch slices fresh ginger

Put all the ingredients into a small pot, bring to a simmer, then cover and let steep overnight. Strain out the spices and store in the refrigerator.

Makes about 1/2 cup

Crème Fraîche

Crème fraîche is similar to sour cream, but it's richer and less tangy. It can be expensive to buy, but why would you since it is so simple to make?

1 cup heavy cream
1 Tbsp buttermilk

Add the buttermilk to the cream and let stand, covered, at room temperature between 1 - 3 days depending on how thick and tangy you like it, then refrigerate. Use within a week or so.

Bouquet Garni

This is just shorthand for a bundle of herbs, in particular parsley (3 - 4 stems), thyme (2 springs), and bay leaf (1 - 2, fresh or dried). Tieing them all together makes it easier to get them out of the pot later on.

Resources

Here's a list of the producers whose ciders or spirits I've used to develop the cocktail recipes in this book. Don't limit yourself to these, though. There are a lot of great ciders out there.

acecider.com
albemarleciderworks.com
anthemcider.com
aspall.co.uk
drinkcider.com (Blue Mountain)
bluebeecider.com
ciderriot.com
coloradocider.com
edenicecider.com
poverylaneorchards.com
  (Farnum Hill)
finnriver.com
foggyridgecider.com
harvestmooncider.com
hennys.co.uk
ninepincider.com
origsin.com
theowlsbrew.com
potterscraftcider.com
reverendnatshardcider.com
schilllingcider.com
seattleciderworks.com
spiritworksdistillery.com
tiltedshed.com

2townsciderhouse.com
virtuecider.com
winchesterciderworks.com

Cider Tasting Events

One way to discover great ciders, especially those that might be made locally, is to attend a cider tasting event. Here's where you can get more information on the major ones.

cidersummitNW.com
  (events in WA, OR, CA, and IL)
porethecore.com
ciderdays.org
ciderweek.com
  (events in OR, WA, NY, and VA)

Other Great Resources

ciderguide.com
hardcidernews.com
cydermarket.com
unitedstatesofcider.com
drinkingcider.com
ciderjournal.com
alongcameacider.com

INDEX

applejack 20, 23, 60
apricot cider 19, 57
aquavit 31
Architech's Fancy 35
Barberrian 15
berry cider 15, 28, 46
Berry Storm 15
Black Velvet 32
bourbon 24
Braised Meatballs 42
brandy 11, 16, 23, 60
Celery Root Rémoulade in Endive
    Leaves 53
cherry cider 31, 46
Cherry Chutney Timbale 46
Cider Nectar 16
Cider Poached Shrimp 45
Cidre Royale 32
Cocoa Hop 28
Cot Dreamin' 19
Dried Apricot Chutney 57
Dr. Walker 24
Gen. Harrison's Nog 36
gin 8, 11, 35
Gin Gin Jenny 8
ginger cider 8, 24, 27
Honey Buzz 12
honey cider 12
hopped cider 20, 28
Jersey Lightning 23
J.P. Hill 20
Maggy May 28

Mekong Melody 19
Methodist, The 24
Midnight Sun 31
Mushroom and Walnut Spread 41
Negroni Piegato 35
Onion Confit Canapés 58
Orleans Aperitif Cider 11, 12
Orleans Fizz 11
ouzo 35
pear cider 35
pepper cider 19
pumpkin cider 23
Pumpkin Cider Toddy 23
Rescue Remedy 27
Revolution No. 3 16
Roasted Chicken Rillettes 54
Rose's Smile 11
Ruby Tuesday 12
rum 8, 16, 19, 60
rye 8, 20, 27
Savory Artichokes 49
scotch 20, 24
shochu 27
Spanish Chorizo Bites 50
Spicy Swede 31
Spring Cider Punch 36
Stone Fence 8
stout 32
tequila 28
Ume Hana 27
Virginia Reel 20
vodka 12, 15